Pattern and Form

poems by John Clark Vincent

Cover and interior design by Lisa D. Holmes (Yulan Studio, yulanstudio.com)

Published in Portland, Oregon by Yulan Studio, Inc.
Printed in the United States

First edition
ISBN: 979-8-9863990-0-3

folding cranes

... for klara

when i fold cranes,
my fingers linger on the creases
you once helped me with.

for it was you
who unveiled my memory of
how special new paper feels.

it was you who reminded me
how simple a task it is to
look within a thing and

discover a heart still beating.

Acknowledgements

First and foremost, I would like to acknowledge the love and support of my soulmate and partner in life, Lisa D. Holmes. She not only inspires me each and every day, she also designs and publishes my manuscripts through her graphic design and publishing firm, Yulan Studio, Inc.

I also wish to acknowledge the contribution a brilliant young friend from our neighborhood has made to this collection. Klara Kjome Fischer, who I first met and got to know through occasional conversations across my garden fence during the Covid lockdown, contributed both poems and inspiration to this chapbook. Klara is currently preparing to embark on her university journey. In the *dialogue with klara* series, I wrote the *(j)* stanzas and Klara wrote the *(k)* stanzas.

Finally, I must acknowledge and sincerely thank my friends and fellow writers — Waka T. Brown, Matteo Merenda, Aileen Sheedy, and Linda Bybee Kapfer — who took the time to read my poems (multiple times) and provide insights and feedback which made them better.

Table of Contents

Section I - Poseur Sonnets

Years Later

Who I am in my heart, my one true heart,
which hides when I come round looking for it,
that is who I truly wish to be. That's
the path I can't believe I ever quit.

What could have happened to bury it so
deeply, and carry me so far away
from the only self I could ever be?
What trauma forced my heart to hide that way

and always swallow the pain? Yet it still
wove endless threads through years of strewn debris.
As though it knew the day would arrive when
I would decide, years later, to trace these

same threads back to the path that leads me home...
through countless fields of scattered, broken stone.

Simply By Being

Remember the one that wouldn't grow straight?
Even times when we were forceful or harsh
she was having none of it. In the end
we pulled her up and tossed her on the trash

out back. We simply forgot about her.
Then remember what we found that winter?
Her branches had draped themselves across the
slick, wet moss, shading the soil around her.

Her tiny, perfect leaves were vibrantly
alive. And her fading blossoms had spread
beneath her, mingling her music with earth's
alluring tunes. "Simply by being," you said,

"she's begun to perfectly sing the song
that she alone was hearing all along."

Stowing the Oars

Extinction is coming. Death is coming.
I can smell its breath. So what exactly
am I doing here? What do I live for?
What winds have carried me in from the sea?

I could paddle hard to get as far from
this place as possible, or, I guess I
could simply stow the oars... decide to drift
awhile. There are no currents, and besides,

this cove does have a pleasant feel. Little
wind; clear water. Not what I imagined...
not where I imagined I'd be this close
to sunset. So near to driftwood and sand.

But to be honest, I'm not sure I know
why I'd turn, so I'm choosing not to go.

As Life Flows Through

Each day we are alive, with every
breath we take, our hearts are cracking open.
And though we may not know it, our tears fall
to mingle with the flood of fluid souls

that forever pool around us. But our
emptiness inside will never be filled.
It's not meant to fill. It simply offers
a path for life to pull us in, until

the need we feel is larger than our hearts
can hold. Strangely, we are given so much
love we fear the river pouring through us.
We fear the path that allows us to touch

all that life can be. All that I and you
can be, as our hearts feel life flowing through.

And She Turned Her Gaze Away

Life is love's journey, and every journey
comes to its end. When have we ever closed
any door on our heart and not suffered?
For me, never. I'll be wretched and loath

to leave, even though I know it won't be
mine to decide if I should stay or go.
It is like the time our life's truest love
first smiled then turned away to let us know

that particular journey was over.
But even then a new journey began.
So regardless how fearful I might be,
I will learn to love again if I can

let myself step into the flow of life,
and just let go of what was never mine.

The Thing I Offer You

I've nothing to offer you but my heart.
What else could there be? I'm too old for games
of chance or anything else that peaks out
doors or hides at the edge of window frames.

There is not enough time left for me to
give anything less than that, you see, and
that requires something solid as stone.
There can be no more castles built of sand.

And my heart... my heart has been tempered with
the ice and flame and joy and pain of love.
A lifetime of it. It's eternal now.
Like the earth below and the sky above.

Oh, can't you see? The thing I offer you
is honesty. I promise you my truth.

The Art of Weaving

The more tea brews, the more astringent it
becomes. But choosing mild over bitter
is not a moral choice. For one is not
good and the other bad. I just prefer

the milder one. You might savor an edge.
And either way is fine with tea as long
as we agree to hear the song it sings.
The story that it shares before it's gone

is how it weaves itself into the web,
the great interwoven web of stories
that binds the tea and me and every bit
of life into what's called eternity.

All stories sing, regardless which choices
we make. And listening brings such joy.

Winter Approaches

Cold rain has fallen five or six days now,
and leaves once vibrant fade into the mud
or swelling moss that clings to everything,
leaving no hope my dreams of warm sun could

survive this fading light that now descends
upon us, whispering that death is real.
Of course, I knew that already. Because
life has never worried how we might feel,

and so it shows us death every damn day.
Yesterday it showed me a young grey fawn.
Other highlights include both rat and wren.
But it's not out to bury everyone...

at least not all of us at the same time...
because for life a sequence works just fine.

Section II - Wistful Waka

the garden path

i garden to live,
quietly as possible,
among small beauties
woven one to another,
sharing everything they are...

passing through

a leaf falls; a perch
darts to the top of the pond...
the ripples extend
as the maples sway less dense
and my thoughts pass freely through.

dialogue with klara I

paper crane *(j)*

a paper crane sits
beneath my dormant dogwood.
perfectly folded,
content with where it now rests.
it seeks no other garden.

garden *(k)*

sky-high mustard greens
grace the earth with their presence.
no wonder it is
heaven to the crane's eyes, perched
where a letter will soon come.

waiting *(j)*

many cranes must fly
to follow the path of life.
but some find a home
in the garden's solitude,
where they've learned to wait in peace.

dialogue with klara II

late winter songs *(j)*

the yellow crocus
burst forth from the dropping snow.
their yearning to sing
lifts them above whatever
challenges life offers them.

change *(k)*

it is odd to think
of bitter winds winding down,
of earth awakened.
yet the flower-sun insists
i will soon feel the earth's turn.

dialogue with klara III

serenity *(j)*

two cranes patiently
rest beneath winter's remains
(a lean-to of twigs,
dried grass, and brown brittle leaves)
waiting to be welcomed home.

back-door awning *(k)*

leaves ward off the rain
at an entrance to my nest
once — still — inviting
but now, too, is the air fresh.
soon, feathers take to sky...where?

what do you hear? *(j)*

some cranes never fly.
others live to breathe the sky.
where each goes depends
upon the songs its heart sings,
and how well it understands.

dialogue with klara IV

self care *(j)*

harmony begins
with the balance inside us...
our sun and our moon
must allow each other to
follow its true path through life.

awareness *(k)*

the challenge for each:
to not eclipse the other,
and recognize the
gentle touch of gravity
as loving guide through life's dance.

a mi amigo

by klara kjome fischer

cuando te veo
en el jardín, diría
que eres ciempiés.
yendo paso a paso,
cultivas diez mil vidas.

pero tu mente,
es como mariposa —
baila en el sol,
milagro de la vida:
unes aire y suelo.

challenges of the heart

our hearts flow through life
looking for nothing but love,
and they never fail...
it's just that we don't always
understand the truth we feel.

da capo

... for sadie

there are times i wish
we could sing your song again...
i would call your name
watch as my voice reaches you,
then feel your joy as you turn.

ongoing feud

each day, some neighbor's
cat shits in my veggie sprouts.
i now hate that cat.
i may come to hate all cats...
i refuse to meditate.

Section III - Acrostic Memories

Discovering Frog Eggs

"Don't bother with boots," my mother said.
"It's going to be waist deep for you."
She spoke of our vegetable garden... the one now
Covered with a couple feet of water. Sometime
Overnight the river we thought of as a neighbor had
Ventured over to visit and clearly planned to stay awhile.
Even the pepper plants were completely submerged, and
Right or wrong, my mother intended to harvest what she could.
I didn't mind a bit. To be honest, I loved it.
Not the harvest. I loved wading through that immense
Garden lake and exploring a new underwater world.

"For starters, pick the peppers," my mother said, so I
Reached for a large green bell right in front of me, and...
Oh my god! What my hand encountered was the most
Gooey, unsettling, gelatinous surprise...

"Eggs," my mother said. "Those are frog eggs," she added,
Grinning at my quick recoil and distasteful grimace.
"Go ahead and skip that one," she continued, "but you
Sure don't seem to mind picking up tadpoles."

The Beauty Of Butterflies

The broken pump behind our old garage, dripping water and
Hidden between two elms, was where I'd often go as a child to
Evade attention. I could hide there forever it seemed.

But that one especially warm Spring day...
Early April I think it was...
Although I suppose it could have been May...
Understand, please, that I'm old now, and
Those types of details elude me, which I'm sure
You'll come to understand, as we all must.

Over the years, it's common for memories to
Fade. So few manage to make it all the way through.

But the day I discovered butterflies will live with me
Until I entirely cease to be. Until
Time itself fades away. Because they
Took a day, one like any other day, and injected an
Electric sort of love into the air.
Right before my eyes, beauty itself began to
Fly all around me. Alighting here or
Landing over there. Fluttering with joy
Into and out of the reach of my hands, but never my
Eyes... I could see them then as I
See them now... and every time, I feel like I too can fly.

Picking Asparagus

Pretty much every Spring when I was growing up,
I would see people searching through the trees —
Cottonwoods mostly — east of our house.
Knives would occasionally flash down,
Indicating a find, a harvest of sorts.
Not much was taken, but something
Got carried away as they returned to waiting cars.

As I watched, I couldn't help being curious
So I asked my father what they were doing.
"Picking wild asaragus," he said.
"Asparagus grows in all the shelter belts
Round here. Birds spread the seeds."
And now, looking back, I realize some
Grand lessons were being handed down to me.
Understanding those lessons did take time, but
Still, they were important lessons nonetheless.

Shorter Modern Poems

So much of our life, both sorrow and joy, depends upon
How ably our hearts can open, and remain so, to each special
Opportunity we encounter along the way... and how quickly we
Recognize our truth in the music being played.
That special opportunity was what Aunt Velma offered me.
Every time I saw her, it seemed to me, she would
Refer to feeding my gift — a comment I never understood.

Most of the time I guessed she must have thought me smart.
Often she gave me books to read. Toynbee... Camus. I
Did read them, but at the age of ten or twelve, I could not grasp
Everything for which I reached. But Velma didn't care.
"Read this," she'd say, then hand me another one. And it was
Not just prose she offered. She shared her jazz, her art, her

Poetry. And somehow, David Morton's *Shorter Modern Poems*
Overcame the obstacles we faced... my life, Velma's death, and
Every other effort to break the channel that flowed between us.
Morton's anthology sits on my shelf now. And when I lift the cover, it
Says, in lovely script... *Velma E. Vincent, Sept. 16 - 1932.*

White Dwarf Stars

When I was twelve, Mr. Reed, my eighth grade science teacher —
He would resurface some years later as my high school principal —
Insisted that all stars were larger than planets. And when I
Told him he was wrong, he was not happy. But I often read
Encyclopedias in those days, and I'd read about white dwarf stars.

Discovering he was wrong wasn't easy for him, because he
Was embarrassed. I meant him no harm. For it was not my
Aim to be hurtful. I just wanted him to know the truth. Was I
Right to do what I did? Was my mother right to deny me the
Freedom to get a library card and read what I wanted? Would

Some other path for all of us have changed things? Who knows. But
To me, what's important to know is the fact that dwarf stars are real.
And the need to speak the truth is real. And our choice to
Read and write and sing and pray and work and play and
Say the things that need to be said will never ever go away.

Learning To Square Dance

Let's see... there was Sarah, of course, and Martha, and Martha's
Elder brother, David. Rosemary, Jim, and Jolene...
And, besides me, one other boy I can't remember... at least not
Right now. I hope that name surfaces later. But right
Now, what I'm focused on is how much fun it always was to
Involve myself with that wonderful circle of friends.
Nothing mattered on the evenings we practiced except
Getting the steps down right; and soaking in the happy anticipation

That overtook everyone present. It literally pulled the laughter
Out of each of us during this first foray into the world of dancing.

Square dancing was a beginning of sorts. An opportunity to
Quietly, almost secretly, learn how it felt to hold a girl's hand. How
Unusually stirring it was to place your hand on your partner's lower back,
And, holding fast to one another, oh so freely swing. The
Rules were designed, it seemed, to open our thoughts to possibilities
Even greater than those we could imagine in our early adolescent days.

Dancing would evolve for me over the years. I had classes in ballroom
And folk. Watched ballet and interpretive art. And I rocked around the clock.
Never once did dancing feel less than beautiful. Never once
Could I imagine anything but love emerging from that expression of life.
Even now, looking back, from square dancing till today. It still feels perfect.

After Summer Rain

After a replenishing summer rain, it was common
For a sense of peace to settle in on our small family farm.
Time paused for a little while. It seemed to allow the
Earth to breathe a bit more easily before our country life
Returned to its regular, and necessary, get-it-done pace.

So for a young farmboy like me, who did not yet
Understand life but yearned to do so, those easy
Moments offered needed respite and myriad pools of reflection...
Mud puddles are what some folks called them...
Even so, to me the water caught the quiet light, and
Reflected the endless stream of possibilities waiting in the

River I was beginning to drift down. In those moments,
As I tried to look ahead to a world I could not yet imagine,
I felt completely empty and alone. But the sadness I felt
Never made me want to turn away. I knew what I felt was me.

www.ingramcontent.com/pod-product-compliance
Lightning Source LLC
Chambersburg PA
CBHW030528130626
46549CB00007B/3150